Understanding
Fish Oils

FIRST STONE

Contents

1 Why Are Fish Oils Special?

Fish oils are big news these days. Traditionally, fish has always been thought of as brain food (with, it turns out, plenty of justification), but now every article you read proclaims their benefits for a wide range of ailments including arthritis, hyperactivity, asthma, heart health, skin conditions and some cancers.

Can such a superfood really exist? The answer is "yes". The oils contained in abundance in the flesh of many types of fish have a profound effect on human health.

Diets that are typically high in omega-3 fish oils, such as those of the Japanese, Inuit (Eskimos) and the Mediterranean countries, tend to have low levels of certain diseases. It was this that first alerted researchers to the possibility that fish oils might be highly beneficial.

SPECIAL FATS

The fatty acids found in fish oils are particularly important nowadays for two reasons:

- They are biologically very active and are used in nervous tissue and cell membrane structure, as well as being important for keeping inflammation down and keeping blood thinned.
- The family of fats to which they belong, the omega-3s, do not make up a significant part of the modern diet as they did in previous times. In other words, we are not eating enough of them.

The naturally occurring oils found in fish contain special types of polyunsaturated fats. Because the oils have a low freezing temperature, they are useful for fish, which need to remain flexible yet swim in cold waters.

If the oils in their flesh hardened at cold temperatures (like butter hardening in the fridge), the fish would be rigid and would be unable to swim!

These fats are particularly beneficial to human health, and are protective against a wide range of ailments. This is because of their unique chemical structures, which are of particular importance for

The chemical structure of fish oils is beneficial to human health.

brain and nerve structure, as anti-inflammatory agents, and to promote anti-blood clotting factors. The fluidity of these fats is what makes them so biologically active for us as well as for fish.

It is thought that we evolved on a diet that was high in these fats, which is why they are of

7

such importance to us. Modern diets, which are deficient in these fats, can be directly linked to the high incidences of a variety of health problems.

A BASIC OUTLINE OF FATS

To understand more, it is necessary to explain a little bit about fats in general. There are three main groups of fats:

SATURATED

Mainly found in meat, milk, cheese and butter. The Western diet typically provides too much of these types of fats.

Hydrogenated fats: These are manufactured fats, used for making cheap margarine. They are used in most commercial baked goods. They can also be thought of as saturated fats (but may, in fact, be more damaging).

MONO-UNSATURATED

These are mainly found in olive oil, and are also called omega-9. Mono-unsaturated fats are a familiar part of the Mediterranean diet.

Olive oil is linked to many health benefits, especially heart health. While not 'biologically active', omega-9 fats may have benefits simply by displacing saturated fats in the diet. (If you are dunking your bread in olive oil, you are not spreading butter on it.)

POLY-UNSATURATED
These fats can be subdivided into two main groups:

Omega-6: Found mainly in cooking oils, grains, seeds and nuts. While particular members of the omega-6 group of fatty acids are valuable for optimal health, modern diets tend to be high in this family of fats because of the amount of cooking oils used, plus the oils used in food processing and convenience foods.

Omega-3: Found in small quantities in some nuts and seeds, in the oil they produce, and in soya. Particularly active types of omega-3s, called EPA and DHA, are found in high quantities in oily fish.

2

The Secret of Fish Oils

This section may, at first, seem a little complicated, but read on – it is fairly straightforward, and is crucial to understanding about fish oils.

The secret of why fish oils are beneficial to human health lies in their specific structure, which is not shared by oils from any other source. All fats and oils are chains made up of links of carbon.

SATURATED

Those carbon chains that are 'saturated' with hydrogen are called saturated fats. The carbon chains tend to be shorter – between 4 and 18 links in the chain – although there are a couple that are longer.

UNSATURATED

These are fatty acids with carbon chains that have spaces, which are missing links to hydrogen. They are, therefore, not 'saturated' with hydrogen, and are called unsaturated. (When fats are hydrogenated or rehydrogenated, the manufacturers are artificially adding hydrogen to saturate the chain). These chains have at least 18 links in the chain. One of the mono-unsaturated fats is shorter with 16 links.

ESSENTIAL FATTY ACIDS

Two 18-link fats are called 'essential fatty acids' because we are unable to make them for ourselves, and we must get them from our diet.

These two essential fats are:

- Alpha-linolenic acid: This is the one we are able to convert in our bodies to the 'fish-oil-type' fats.
- Linoleic acid: This is made by the body into GLA, or gamma-linolenic acid, which many people buy in evening primrose or borage/starflower capsules.

FISH FATTY ACIDS

The magical qualities of fish oils come from the fact that they are very unsaturated. In other words, they have lots of spaces without hydrogen on the chain. They have 20-22 links in the chain, which allows them to have more unsaturated spaces. The degree of unsaturation makes them very flexible, and highly biologically active.

The body can make these 20- to 22-link, highly unsaturated, fats from shorter 18-link fatty acids, but is sometimes inefficient at doing this.

By eating oily fish, you benefit from all the work the fish has already done in converting the fats in its diet (derived from plankton and smaller marine animals), and your body then does not need to make this conversion.

There are three types of fatty acids that are of particular benefit to us, and that are in fish oils:

EPA: eicosapentaenoic acid. This has important anti-inflammatory effects, and helps to reduce blood 'stickiness'.

DHA: docosahexaenoic acid. This is important for nerve and brain health.

AA: arachidonic acid. This is important for eye health.

FISH IN THE DIET
The best way we can improve our diet is to eat more oily fish. Eating about 100g/4oz of oily

13

Mackerel: High in oil.

fish will, on average, give you about 2g of fish oils. It is important to bear in mind that white fish has very low levels of these beneficial oils.

The following tables give average levels of omega-3 fats in various fish:

FISH WITH HIGH AMOUNTS OF OILS:
1.5-3.5G PER 100G/4OZ PORTION
Tuna (fresh)
Mackerel (fresh – or smoked has over 6g per 100g)
Salmon (fresh or smoked)

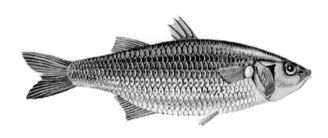

Grey Mullet: High in oil.

Sardines (fresh or canned)	Mullet
Herrings	Sprats
Anchovies	Sturgeon
Pink trout	Eel.
Kippers	

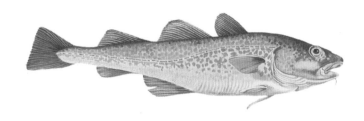

Cod: Low in oil.

FISH WITH MEDIUM AMOUNTS OF OILS: *0.5-1.5G PER 100G/4OZ PORTION*

Halibut

Smelt

Shark

Oyster

Swordfish

Trout.

FISH WITH LOW AMOUNTS OF OILS: *LESS THAN 0.5G PER 100G/4OZ PORTION*

Tuna (canned, vegetable oil drained or water packed)

Halibut: Medium oil content.

Bass
Bream
Cod
Coley
Prawns
Mussels
Haddock
Oysters.

FINDING THE BALANCE
Achieving a balance of fatty
acids in our diet seems to be
the main problem we
encounter.

In general, it is advised that
we should get around 30 per
cent of our total calorie intake

from fats from our diet. This is compared to a typical intake in Western cultures of 35-40 per cent.

Of this ideal 30 per cent, we should be getting no more than one-third saturated fats, and two-thirds should be unsaturated (polyunsaturated and also mono-unsaturated).

Of the polyunsaturated fats, it seems that we are now typically eating a ratio of about 16:1 omega-6 to omega-3. Compare

These days the customer is offered a wider range of fish than ever before.

this with the ratio of 2:1, or even 1:1, that our ancestors would have eaten, and you can see how unbalanced our diets have become.

Part of the reason for this imbalance is our heavy dependence on commercially prepared convenience foods. The food manufacturers like to use stable fats, and so they use hydrogenated omega-6 fats in their products, as well as oils that are very high in omega-6, such as corn oil.

In the meantime, our consumption of sources of omega-3 – from fish and game (free-feeding, grass-grazing animals), plus plant sources – has declined to a fraction of what it once was.

It is this ratio imbalance, which has accelerated dramatically in the last 100 years, that is contributing to the wide variety of health problems we now experience.

SHELF-LIFE
Some manufacturers now recognise the implications of an unbalanced diet, and they are

19

enhancing some foods with omega-3s. For example, eggs are now available from chickens that have been fed high omega-3 diets, and work is being done to stabilise the omega-3 oils and include them in other foods.

However, the instability of the fats – which makes them so biologically valuable – is the worst enemy of food manufacturers, who need products with a long shelf-life.

Fish oils go rancid quite quickly on exposure to air, which accounts for their funny smell when fish goes off.

However, when fish is really fresh, it hardly smells at all. This can be borne out by a visit to a Japanese fish market, as the Japanese are scrupulous about the freshness of their fish.

HOW MUCH FISH SHOULD I EAT?

We certainly need to improve our average intake of fish. Consumption has dropped by 50 per cent since the 1950s. In the UK, we now eat the equivalent of just one portion a week, and most of this is in the form of non-oily white fish, such as cod. This is generally in the form of fish and chips, and fishfingers.

Official government dietary advice is that we need to eat two portions of fish a week (a portion is about 100-150g/4-6oz). Of these two portions, one needs to be oily fish (see page 14), and one can be low-fat white fish.

However, a nutritionist interested in 'optimal health' will advocate that if you are seeking to prevent heart disease, certain cancers, and alleviate arthritis and allergic conditions, you may need to eat three meals of oil-rich seafood weekly. If this level of consumption presents problems, then fish oil supplements may be a useful option (see page 30).

WHAT ABOUT NON-FISH EATERS?

For people who do not eat fish, there is the option of taking fish oil supplements. If you do not want to do this, you can get other members of the omega-3 oil family of fatty acids from alternative sources. These include:

- Flax oil – one of the best sources
- Walnuts
- Soya
- Linseeds (freshly cracked to liberate the oils)
- Canola/rape oil (does not taste terrific, but can be combined with olive oil).

However, these plant sources of omega-3 are slightly different from fish oils. They need to be converted in the human body into the types of oils we have been discussing, and which are found in abundance in oily fish.

The conversion of the essential fatty acid ALA (alpha-linolenic acid) can be inefficient, and may be poor in some people, particularly those from atopic, allergy-prone, families. It seems that the fatty acids will convert relatively easily into EPA, which are useful for skin health and as an anti-inflammatory, but not very readily into DHA, which is important for nerve functioning.

If you wish to use these sources, they will do some good, but they may not be as beneficial as you would wish in some instances.

Certain factors can easily interfere with the conversion of ALA into EPA/DHA, and it is best to moderate these as far as possible. They include:

- A high amount of omega-6 fats in the diet. (These compete directly with ALA for the enzymes which are responsible for the conversion process.)
- A high amount of saturated fat in the diet
- Too much alcohol
- Smoking.

3 Problems of Pollution

If there is a downside to increasing your consumption of oily fish, it is in the potential for increasing your intake of some pollutants.

However, a sensible approach can minimise this risk. There are two main areas of concern:

INDUSTRIAL POLLUTANTS
This relates to PCBs (Poly-chlorinated Biphenyls), dioxins, and other related chemicals that find their way into our waters and that affect fish. This is often because of chemical run-off into rivers, which, in turn, finds its way into sea waters.

The principal concerns are farmed fish, which are found in coastal waters, and salmon, which are the most extensively farmed fish. Additionally, the feed they are given is thought to be a source of these chemicals. While dioxin output is now strictly controlled in many Westernised countries, developing countries still are not restricting them.

The fears about these chemicals are varied, but mainly centre on their potential as

Try to eat wild-caught fish rather than farmed fish.

hormone disrupters. The amount in one portion of oily fish a week is probably acceptable, unless you are pregnant (or planning a pregnancy), or you are a small child. But according to many experts, the health benefits of fish oils in these circumstances probably outweigh the disadvantages.

If you can afford it, it may be prudent to eat wild fish instead of farmed fish. It is also important to put the danger of pollution into perspective in terms of the whole diet. By far the greatest source of these chemicals is dairy produce, which we actively promote during pregnancy and childhood, and fish ranks second to this, alongside meat.

If you reduce these other sources in the diet in favour of increasing fish consumption, you also experience other health benefits, such as reducing saturated fat levels.

Calcium is available from many other dietary sources, apart from dairy, including fortified soya, rice and oat milks; green, leafy vegetables; sprouts;

bread; nuts; seeds; eggs; raisins (and other dried fruit); and sardines.

MERCURY

The toxic heavy metal mercury has been found in certain types of deep-water fish. The fish to cause particular concern are shark, swordfish, marlin and tuna. Mercury is naturally present in sea water, and is also dumped from industrial processes. The bacteria in sea water turns it into its worst form, methyl mercury. Because the aforementioned fish are predators, the small amounts in the tissues of smaller fish become concentrated in them.

Mercury is responsible for nerve damage, particularly in developing children (it is the use of mercury by hatmakers that inspired the Mad Hatter character in Lewis Carroll's *Alice in Wonderland*).

The advised maximum intake of fish affected by mercury is 140g/4.9oz a week, or about an average portion. In practice, most people do not eat this much of these particular species (with the exception of tuna), and so it makes sense to vary the source of oily fish you consume. In particular, it may be advisable to limit your intake of these sources if you are pregnant and for children (who can experience a lower toxic level as their body sizes are proportionately smaller).

Pregnant women are advised, now, to avoid shark, swordfish and marlin completely, due to their mercury levels. Tuna has less mercury and pregnant women are advised to limit tuna to one medium steak of fresh fish or two cans of tuna per week. Other oily fish are fine – for instance, salmon, sardines and mackerel are excellent alternatives.

Another possibility is to take supplements, which are guaranteed to contain low levels of this metal.

Fish oils are still of tremendous benefit during pregnancy and childhood (see page 42) and getting the balance right at this time is of great importance.

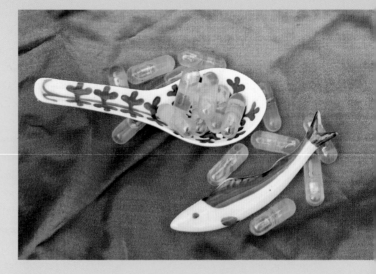

4 Fish Oil Supplements

There are several possible reasons why you might decide to take fish oil supplements:

- If you do not eat enough oily fish in your diet
- If you need to consume high doses for a particular therapeutic effect (for example to help reduce the symptoms of arthritis or asthma)
- If you are concerned about pollution levels in fish.

DOSAGE LEVELS
A typical, good-quality supplement will provide 1,000mg (one gram) of fish oils. Depending on the brand, they will deliver between 150-350 mg of EPA, and 100-220 mg DHA. Some brands also combine fish oils with borage oil (or the less potent evening primrose oil) to give a balanced mix with GLA. All supplements should be formulated with antioxidants, such as vitamin E, to help prevent rancidity.

The dose suggestion is one to two capsules daily (more is unlikely to provide benefit). Capsules are usually made of

31

gelatine as this used to be the only way to encapsulate oils. A process is now available which does not use gelatine.

CAN YOU OVERDOSE?

As with any supplement, it is advisable to stick within the suggested dosage levels. However, as fats are a 'macronutrient' (along with protein and carbohydrates, they are needed in large amounts in the diet, unlike vitamins which are micronutrients), the tolerance range is quite high.

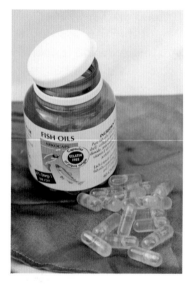

When taking supplements, stick within the suggested dosage levels.

The only instances where caution might be needed is if you are taking anti-coagulant, blood-thinning, medication (see page 38), if an operation is planned, or if you are about to give birth, when excessively thinned blood might be a concern. In these cases, stick to dietary fish oil intake, and moderate supplements for a while.

COD LIVER OIL

Cod liver oil was once a popular dietary supplement – as many long-suffering children of earlier generations can testify. However, this form of taking fish oil has become less popular recently.

The reason for this is that the liver is a very rich source of vitamins A and D. If you need these nutrients, cod liver oil is a very appropriate source. However, children, pregnant women (or those who are likely to become pregnant), and those taking multiple sources of supplements need to be very careful for the following reasons:

- In children, there is a danger

of overdosing on vitamins A and D, which are stored in the body and can build up. While these nutrients are vital for children, and often included in child-formulated supplements, too much can be a bad thing.

- In pregnancy, vitamin A levels need to be controlled as it could adversely affect the foetus. Therefore, cod liver oil (as well as other liver products, such as pâté) are restricted.

- It is important to check the overall nutrient intake from supplements. If you are taking a multi-vitamin with vitamin A and D in it, as well as an antioxidant supplement with vitamin A in its formula, it is easy to overdose by adding in cod liver oil, which is also rich in vitamins A and D.

- In all of the above instances, it would be better to take fish oil supplements instead of cod liver oil supplements.

- If your reason for taking cod liver oil is to obtain EPA or DHA, it is important to realise that a typical supplement has about half of these fatty acids when compared to supplements labelled 'fish oil', which are taken from the muscle meat and skin of the fish, and which declare the amount of these fatty acids on the side of the package.

- The liver is the organ of detoxification and so, as we live in a more polluted world, there is concern that the liver oils are particularly concentrated sources of substances such as PCBs and dioxins.

5 Therapeutic Uses of Fish Oils

Now we move on to look at the therapeutic uses of fish oils in helping to ease various complaints.

ARTHRITIS

Fish oils have an excellent track record for improving the painful symptoms of arthritis.

They have been found to affect the production of a compound called COX (cyclo-oxygenase) in the same way as pharmaceutical, anti-inflammatory compounds, but without causing gastro-intestinal upset.

One of the other benefits of increasing fish consumption in the diet is that it automatically replaces meat and cheese. These foods are both high in the diets of many people, and they contain fats that are pro-inflammatory and so aggravate arthritic conditions. Eating more fish helps to correct the balance.

HEART DISEASE

Fish oils can help to lower heart disease risk in several ways. DHA is critical for vascular health, while EPA controls blood clotting, artery spasm, lowers unhealthy LDL-cholesterol levels, and lowers triglycerides (total blood fats).

One of the main fish fatty acids, EPA, is involved in the synthesis in the body of a group of compounds called thromboxanes. These compounds have strong anti-coagulation effects, meaning that they stop red blood cells from clumping together. This makes them very powerful for reducing the risk of heart disease as they help to keep blood thin and flowing.

While prevention is always better than cure, studies have also shown a benefit for those after a coronary incident. A study recently presented to the American Heart Association annual conference, based on about 12,000 people who had suffered heart attacks in the previous three months, showed that supplementing fish oils lowered the risk of death significantly.

If you are already on blood-thinning medication, you will need to tell your doctor that you are increasing your oily fish

Fish oils in the diet help to prevent heart disease.

intake or taking capsules so that you can be monitored. In fact, you may well find that the suggestion to eat more fish comes from your doctor, as most are aware of the benefits.

There are other blood-thinning agents, including vitamin E, garlic, and ginseng, and the combination of high doses of these with fish oils might be very powerful, so it is always best to consult your doctor in these instances. Do not stop, or reduce, prescribed medication without consulting your doctor.

DRY SKIN CONDITIONS

Fish oils are beneficial for dry skin conditions, such as eczema, allergies and psoriasis. This is because of the role of the fatty acids in cell membrane structure, and also because of their anti-inflammatory action.

In many instances, flax oil will do as well, as this delivers the omega-3 compounds from which EPA are made. About one tablespoon of flax oil a day for an adult is recommended (although sometimes two tablespoons are needed). Add the flax oil to salad dressings or use it to dress vegetables, but do not use it to cook with. Remember, some people do not make the necessary conversion easily, and if flax oil does not produce results, fish oils can often provide the answer.

It takes at least six weeks for skin cells to replace themselves, and so this is the earliest time to expect results.

ASTHMA

Fish oils are particularly of benefit to asthmatics. Asthma involves the production of inflammatory compounds called LTB4 and LTC4. These lead to breathlessness and discomfort. The leukotrienes that lead to inflammation are 1,000 times more potent than histamine. The omega-3 fats in oily fish have been found significantly to reduce the production of these irritants, and improve lung function. Children who eat oily fish have significantly less asthma.

Patience is needed, as eating oily fish regularly or taking supplements will probably not have a therapeutic effect for at least 18 weeks. Again, reducing sources of saturated fats and hydrogenated fats is likely to improve this effect.

PREGNANCY AND BREAST FEEDING

DHA found in fish oils is vital for brain development in babies. It is also thought that fish oils are responsible for making us more intelligent.

In the foetus, 70 per cent of the energy that crosses the placenta is devoted to brain growth, and the brain continues to 'branch' and develop well into the first two years after birth. The nutrients available for this process are very important. The most important times for these fats are in the last trimester, and in the first three months of life.

It is a telling fact that the only time that the human body is able to manufacture certain essential fats in abundance is in breast milk, which indicates the importance of some fats to the infant who cannot yet obtain them from their diet.

Now formula milks are being supplemented with some of these fats, as there is evidence

DHA in fish oils is vital for brain development in babies.

that bottle-fed babies do not do as well in cognitive development and eye health as do breast-fed babies, who automatically get these fats. However, the technology, type and quantities of these fats can still be improved in formula milks. Breast is still best from this point of view.

Studies prove that populations who eat more fish suffer less from depression.

helpful (possibly in lowering the risk of pre-eclampsia), but it is also true that there can be greater blood loss during delivery. Therefore, it may be advisable to reduce your supplement intake in the last month of pregnancy, and to rely instead on dietary intake.

MOODS AND DEPRESSION

DHA in fish oils seems to be very important for regulating brain function. The brain is actually made up of 60 per cent fat, and the make-up of fats in the diet has a real impact on

However, there is one potential problem with supplements and pregnancy, which should be considered. This is the effect they have on blood thinning, which may be

mental health. DHA is used directly in brain and nerve structure.

A total of 22 million prescriptions are written for antidepressants each year in the UK, costing nearly £300 million a year. Cross-cultural studies suggest a strong relationship between the types of fatty acids consumed in different cultures, and their rates of depression.

For example, in New Zealand 18kg of fish is eaten annually and six per cent of the population is affected by depression. In Japan, 64kg is eaten per year, and less than one per cent of the population is affected by depression. This correlation is mirrored across the world.

When a Western diet of processed and fried foods is adopted by non-Western cultures, depression rates rise. There may well be other elements of Westernisation that contribute, but fish oils seem to be a strong factor.

HYPERACTIVITY AND LEARNING DIFFICULTIES

One of the most exciting areas

in which fish oils are having a profound impact is that of children with learning and behavioural disorders.

The tendency, these days, is to medicate children, but, by supplying fish oils, you can get to the root of the problem. This will improve the quality of life for the child, as well as for the whole family. It may take up to three months to see a difference, but about 60 per cent of cases improve partially or dramatically with supplementation.

Dietary fish is helpful, but getting a child to eat fish if they are not used to it can be awkward for some parents. Also, the amounts needed would mean eating oily fish daily. For this reason, taking supplements is often more practical.

Fish oil supplements are perfectly safe for children, though it is best to steer clear of cod liver oil.

This gives lower levels of EPA/DHA, and can lead to toxic levels of vitamins A and D when given to children in large quantities.

BREAST, PROSTATE AND COLON HEALTH

Research is showing that diets rich in oily fish can help to protect against breast and prostate cancers.

Even more exciting than this, early reports of trials are suggesting that when fish oils are added into the diet, the signs of these cancers and tumours regress.

This means that they may have important therapeutic effects.

One expert has said: "There is great potential for fish oils in preventing cancer, and a high intake is associated with a reduction in risk of certain cancers, including breast, prostate and colon cancers. It is also clear from laboratory studies that fish oils can reduce the rate of tumour growth if cancer does occur."

6 Case Histories

Jennifer describes a long journey to discover what was troubling her son Jake, now aged six. After much searching, eventually she saw real progress after using fish oils on a daily basis.

"Jake would scream non-stop, and only slept for about four hours in a 24-hour period," said Jennifer. "I was told he had colic initially, but finally the doctors decided that he had 'spectrum disorder', a mildly autistic range that includes dyspraxia (severe clumsiness, which probably has a neurological basis), and ADHD (attention deficit hyperactivity disorder).

"We were confused all along the way because he met so many of his 'markers' early on. Jake walked at 8-9 months and was potty-trained at 15 months. But his speech was slow and he made no eye contact. During

49

therapy sessions, he needed sensory input all the time. He needed to be touched a lot, but communication and motor skills remained frustratingly slow to develop.

"Someone mentioned fish oils to me, and I was half really hopeful and half really sceptical about the idea."

After starting Jake on fish oils at about the age of five, Jake's teacher noticed improvements in about a month (which is quite a short period of time).

He was sitting better in class during story time and not rolling around. He could begin to write short sentences with his finger. His confidence has grown as a result, and he even is able to argue with the referee during football matches (something not all parents would welcome but which was manna from heaven for Jennifer). He talks to strangers, makes eye contact and touches people – all of which would simply not happen previously.

A really wonderful moment happened when a neighbour came to call. She had known Jake since he was born, but he had never acknowledged her. Suddenly, after a couple of months of the fish oils, he suddenly said: "Hello, Mrs P", and walked off!

After a year of taking fish oils, Jake has experienced consistent improvements, and is now much more fully integrated with his peer group.

Sally, aged 52, became progressively affected by arthritis. She had gone from playing tennis twice a week and enjoying walking her dog on most days, to finding the tennis near impossible, and the walks less manageable.

To make things worse, the anti-inflammatory medication she was prescribed was causing stomach upset sufficient for internal bleeding. She had to change prescription and take iron supplements as she had become anaemic.

> *The one remedy that seemed to have no downsides was fish oil supplements*

"I was becoming pretty desperate," said Sally. "I had always considered myself fairly fit and enjoyed being active, but I was beginning to get a little depressed about the prospect of a restricted life. It was not what I had planned at all!

"I started reading about the subject, and the one remedy that seemed to have no downsides, and that everyone was really enthusiastic about, was fish oil supplements.

"It sort of made sense to me because I had been given cod

liver oil as a child (head back, nose pinched, and swallow quickly!) by my mother, and it resonated with me as a good old-fashioned remedy that could work.

"I started making a point of eating oily fish three times a week, and was pleasantly surprised by how much I enjoyed it. I also started taking two fish oil supplements every day.

"It took about six weeks to feel any benefit, but the inflammation started going down noticeably, and my joints felt a lot more free.

"I am not quite back to tennis yet, which I think would be tempting fate, but I walk very vigorously to make up for it and have no ill effects."

A side benefit, noted recently by her doctor, is that Sally's slightly elevated blood pressure has also gone down into the normal range.

7 Serving Ideas

Most fish dishes are quick and easy to prepare – they could almost be described as the healthiest form of fast food.

Indeed, because fish is delicate both in flavour and in terms of the stability of the valuable oils it contains, it should not be overcooked. In the UK, we tend to eat mostly white fish, in the form of fish and chips or fish fingers. However, these are not good sources of the fats we have been discussing.

If you are not used to eating a lot of oily fish, you might find some of these serving suggestions helpful. Apart from grilling, baking and poaching fish, experiment with these ideas:

- A good, basic recipe is to douse the fish in white wine, garlic and herbs, and bake until cooked. You could also add in mushrooms. Alternatively, mix in canned tomatoes and sweet red peppers for a different version.
- Smoked salmon and scrambled eggs is a classic dish.

Mackerel spuds.

- Sardines on toast is the easiest of quick snacks or suppers.
- Meaty fish, such as swordfish fillets, and firm-fleshed fish, such as mackerel fillets or fresh sardines, cook well on the barbecue.
- Mackerel pâté with crudités is a great standby.
- Sweet cured (roll mop) herrings on blinis (buckwheat pancakes) or on toast.
- Kedgeree (haddock with slightly curried rice) takes some time, but is delicious – and not just as a breakfast

Barbecued herrings.

Seafood kebabs.

dish. A fish-based risotto or paella is another option.

- Fish kebabs (use fish with firm flesh), with fresh fruit (such as mango).
- Fishy baked potatoes – stuff with salmon and peas, and top with a herby white sauce.
- Fish cakes or fish pie
- Sushi or sashimi.

Luxury fish pie.

8 Further Information

FURTHER READING

Fats That Heal, Fats That Kill
by Dr Udo Erasmus
Published by Alive Books

The LCP Solution
The Remarkable Nutritional
Answer to ADHD, Dyslexia and
Dyspraxia
by Dr Jacqueline Stordy
Published by Macmillan

TO FIND A NUTRITIONAL THERAPIST

British Association of Nutritional Therapists (BANT)
27 Old Gloucester Street
London WC1N 3XX
Tel. 0870 6061284
www.bant.org.uk

Institute for Optimum Nutrition (ION)
13 Blades Court
Deodar Road
London SW15 2NU
Tel. 020 8877 9993 or
www.ion.ac.uk

USEFUL WEBSITES
www.omega-3info.com
www.seafish.co.uk

About the author

Suzannah Olivier is a nutritionist, health writer and author. She writes regularly for a number of publications, including *The Times*. Her books include:

What Should I Feed My Baby? (Weidenfeld & Nicolson)

The Breast Cancer Prevention and Recovery Diet (Penguin)

The Detox Manual, Banish Bloating, Maximising Energy, Eating for a Perfect Pregnancy, Natural Hormone Balance, Allergy Solutions (all Simon & Schuster Pocket Books)

The Stress Protection Plan (Collins & Brown)

500 of the Most Important Stress Busting Tips You'll Ever Need, 101 Ways to Simplify Your Life (both Cico Books).

Healthy Food for Happy Kids (Simon & Schuster).

Suzannah Olivier's website is www.healthandnutrition.co.uk

Other titles in the series

- **Understanding Acupressure**
- **Understanding Acupuncture**
- **Understanding The Alexander Technique**
- **Understanding Aromatherapy**
- **Understanding Bach Flower Remedies**
- **Understanding Echinacea**
- **Understanding Evening Primrose**
- **Understanding Feng Shui**
- **Understanding Garlic**
- **Understanding Ginseng**
- **Understanding Head Massage**
- **Understanding Kinesiology**
- **Understanding Lavender**
- **Understanding Massage**
- **Understanding Pilates**
- **Understanding Reflexology**
- **Understanding Reiki**
- **Understanding St. John's Wort**
- **Understanding Shiatsu**
- **Understanding Yoga**

First published 2003 by First Stone Publishing
4/5 The Marina, Harbour Road, Lydney, Gloucestershire, GL15 5ET

The publishers would like to thank the Sea Fish Industry Authority for providing the
images for this book.

**The contents of this book are for information only and are not intended as a substitute for
appropriate medical attention. The author and publishers admit no liability for any
consequences arising from following any advice contained within this book. If you have any
concerns about your health or medication, always consult your doctor.**

ISBN 1 904439 05 5

Printed and bound in Hong Kong through Printworks International Ltd.

Understanding
Reflexology

Contents

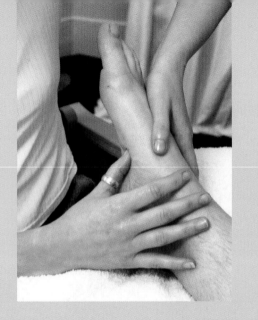

1

Introducing Reflexology

Essentially, reflexology is a specialised form of massage, in which varying degrees of pressure are applied to the feet, and sometimes the hands, in order to produce beneficial effects in other parts of the body.

Like many complementary therapies, reflexology claims some ancient roots. Foot and hand massage or manipulation is thought to have been used in Ancient Chinese, Indian and Egyptian societies. However, whether this was really comparable to modern reflexology is hard to tell.

Modern reflexology owes much of its development to William H. Fitzgerald, a 20th century American ear, nose and throat specialist (see Chapter Two). Other highly significant figures include Eunice Ingham, who published detailed 'maps' of the feet and wrote the highly influential *Stories The Feet Can Tell* and *Stories The Feet Have Told,* and Doreen Bailey, trained by Ingham, who is credited with introducing reflexology to Britain.

5

SOME HEALTH PROBLEMS
THAT MAY BE HELPED BY REFLEXOLOGY

- Aches and pains
- Allergies
- Chronic conditions (such as colic and glue ear in children, and dementia or confusion in the elderly)
- Detoxification
- Digestive problems
- Headaches and migraines
- Infertility (including low sperm count and ovulation irregularities)
- Jetlag
- Menstrual problems
- Pregnancy, labour and postnatal problems
- Progressive disorders (such as multiple sclerosis)
- Sinusitis
- Skin problems
- Stress and anxiety
- Tiredness, fatigue and ME
- Weak immune system
- Wound healing

HEALTH BENEFITS

The aim of reflexology is to improve our general health and sense of well-being. The therapy is suitable for almost everybody, and it is considered very safe. Reflexologists believe it may also help with a range of health problems (see table opposite).

RESEARCH FINDINGS

When the British Reflexology Association, represented by the Reflexology Forum (the profession's regulatory organisation), surveyed its members, it found that 75 per cent of reflexologists believed that their treatments improved or alleviated health problems presented by clients. The most common problems seen by reflexologists were stress, backache and sciatica.

There is plenty of anecdotal and empirical evidence – in the form of case studies written up in professional journals, and patients' experiences published in newspapers and magazines – which suggests that reflexology can successfully treat many different health problems.

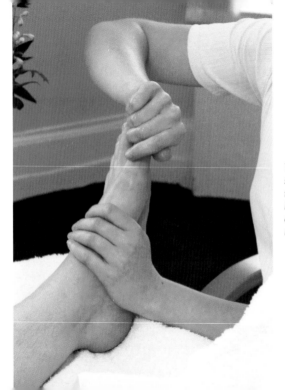

There are many studies suggesting that reflexology can help in the treatment of headaches and migraine.

Unfortunately, there is little scientific evidence to support these claims. Many therapists argue that this is largely due to the fact that complementary therapies such as reflexology cannot easily be tested by randomised, controlled trials. Furthermore, there is often neither the money, nor the expertise, within the profession to devise more appropriate research methods. This may change due to the Government's expansion of complementary research through universities.

Although there are no 'true' clinical, controlled trials, there are numerous studies that suggest reflexology can help to alleviate stress and anxiety, improve feelings of well-being, and treat chronic headaches and migraines. A more rigorous study of the use of ear, hand and foot reflexology in the treatment of pre-menstrual symptoms found that women who received reflexology experienced a much greater improvement in their symptoms than those women who did not.

2 A Brief History

The simple pleasures of putting one's feet up or giving them a gentle rub at the end of a long day are ones our ancient forebears would have enjoyed as much as us.

Taking care of our feet does seem to make our entire body feel good. It is not unreasonable to assume that our ancestors may also have made a connection between this sense of well-being and the process of manipulating the feet. Certainly, there is some evidence, from China and India, dating back more than 5,000 years ago, of the therapeutic use of hand and foot pressure or massage for the treatment of pain and other health problems.

Taking care of our feet does seem to make our entire body feel good.

ARCHAEOLOGY

Archaeologists have found a stone relief and paintings in the tomb of the physician Ankhmahar at Saqqara, Egypt, which suggest that the Ancient Egyptians were using some form of therapeutic manipulation of the feet and hands around 2500-2300 BC.

For example, one pictograph shows two attendants working on the hands and feet of two 'patients'. However, some more sceptical historians have suggested that the attendants are actually giving a manicure rather than a massage!

Some Native American tribes, who believe that our feet are our spiritual connection with the earth, also have a long tradition of foot massage.

ZONE THERAPY

Reflexology as practised today stems largely from the work of William H. Fitzgerald (1872-1942), an American ear, nose and throat specialist. He made the accidental discovery that, if he applied gentle pressure to areas of the hand and foot, he caused partial anaesthesia in the ear, nose and throat. He claimed that his discovery allowed him to perform minor surgery without using a more conventional anaesthetic.

In 1917, Fitzgerald published a paper describing 'reflex zone therapy', a term coined by medical journalist Dr. Edwin Bowers, with whom Fitzgerald co-wrote the paper.

The paper identified 10 longitudinal zones. Each zone ran from each of the five digits of the hand, through the arm, head and body, ending in the corresponding digit of the foot (or running in the opposite direction, i.e. toe to finger). Fitzgerald argued that the zones were of equal width and ran front to back through the body, unlike the meridian zones in traditional Chinese medicine.

Fitzgerald demonstrated an energy link between areas in the same zone. He argued that applying controlled pressure through these 'zones', using either the fingers and thumbs, or devices such as clamps and elastic bands, produced a response elsewhere in the zone. The paper went on to argue that this response could be used to induce an anaesthetic-like state through the zone, allowing minor operations to be performed.

MODERN REFLEXOLOGY

The ground-breaking work pioneered by Fitzgerald was built on by others, who further developed the principles and practice of reflexology.

Fitzgerald's zone therapy ideas attracted the attention of Dr. Joe Riley and his wife, who began to investigate further. They employed a then young Eunice Ingham, who developed Fitzgerald's theory of zones.

Ingham was hugely influential in the development of reflexology. She believed that all parts of the body could be affected by pressure on clearly defined areas of the feet – especially the soles. She developed her own techniques, firstly coining the term 'compression massage' and later 'reflexology'.

Hanne Marquardt, a student of Ingham, later introduced the concept of three horizontal zones, known as 'transverse' zones, which correspond to natural anatomical divisions (shoulder, waist and pelvic floor). With the longitudinal zones first identified by Fitzgerald, these create a grid system for the identification of areas in reflexology.

During the 1960s, another student of Ingham, Doreen Bailey, introduced reflexology to the UK when she opened up a training school for therapists. Since then, the popularity of reflexology has increased steadily.

Within the National Health Service reflexology is also gaining quite a following, particularly among nurses. In GP surgeries, for example, it is being used to treat stress and stress-related problems. On long-stay elderly-care wards and nursing homes, reflexology is being used to help with health problems associated with old age. In cancer care it is regularly used as a complement to conventional treatments.

REFLEXOLOGY SCHOOLS

Over the time in which reflexology has developed, a number of schools teaching new ideas have been established. These include:

- Traditional reflexology
- Holistic, multi-dimensional reflexology
- Morrell reflexology
- Reflex zone therapy
- Rwo shr method
- Vacuflex reflexology.

There are variations between the schools in where the reflexes are said to be located, and, indeed, in the methods of treatment.

Some reflexologists have gone on to develop completely new techniques, based on the principles of conventional reflexology, as, for example, in the case of the metamorphic technique (see opposite). Two examples are described on pages 17-19 to illustrate the variations found in reflexology.

METAMORPHIC TECHNIQUE

This technique was devised in the 1960s, by Robert St. John, a British reflexologist and naturopath. His intention was to help patients to heal themselves.

Originally called 'prenatal' therapy, the metamorphic technique is based on the belief that ill-health can be traced back to problems in the womb. St. John said that, as well as every part of the body being represented on the foot, our time in the womb is also mapped out on the side of the foot, along points known as 'spinal reflexes'.

St. John argues that physical, mental, emotional and spiritual patterns, set before birth, can be felt in the altered states of the foot's surfaces.

Practitioners of the technique use a light, vibratory touch to help their patients release 'energy blockages' and to alter the states that resulted in ill-health or stress.

No one knows how the technique works, but it is believed that the person's own innate intelligence interacts

The metamorphic technique has also been used to help with conditions such as ME, multiple sclerosis and cancer.

VACUFLEX REFLEXOLOGY
Dutch reflexologist Inge Dougans developed this technique in the 1970s. She believed that reflexology worked by treating the meridians (energy pathways in the body) described in traditional Chinese medicine, and devised a method of stimulating all the reflex areas at the same time.

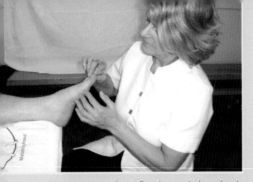

Metamorphic reflexology is believed to be particularly effective at relieving anxiety.

with their lifeforce, brnging beneficial changes at their own rate of growth. Proponents claim great success, particularly for clients who feel that they are 'in a rut' or those who suffer from anxiety.

Patients must wear special vacuflex boots, made of felt, at the beginning of a treatment. The air inside is removed with a vacuum pump, squeezing the feet firmly and stimulating all the reflexes at once.

Vacuflex treatment normally last about five minutes, after which the boots are removed. The therapist immediately examines the feet for areas of discoloration, which are said to correspond to areas of congestion and ill-health. These marks tend to fade after about 30 seconds and progress is measured by changes in these areas over successive treatments.

The second stage of treatment involves the use of silicon pads, which are placed for a few seconds on specific reflex points that lie along energy meridians on the feet, legs, hands and arms. These pads are held in place by gentle suction and are believed to stimulate the meridians.

Proponents of vacuflex reflexology say it is an effective treatment for a wide range of health problems.

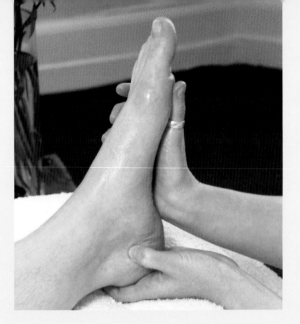

3

How It Works

In reflexology, specific techniques are used, with controlled pressure on the 'reflex areas', usually in the feet or occasionally in the hands.

Reflexologists believe that the extremities of the body (e.g. feet, hands and head) hold information about the whole body. We protect our feet with shoes and socks, which makes our feet highly sensitive. This allows the reflexologist to work deeply and responsively with the feet. Also, the surface area of the sole is quite large, allowing the therapist to work more precisely. Furthermore, the fact that the feet are in frequent contact with the ground means that a stronger link is established with the energy of the planet we inhabit, reaffirming a sense of 'groundedness.'

The reflex areas are said to correspond to particular organs and body parts. A therapist can assess the state of health in every part of the body, and treat accordingly.

One way to explain how

reflexology works is that the appropriate application of pressure to specific reflex points causes a stimulation or relaxation response in the reflected part of the body. This can, therefore, help the body return to a healthy state of balance or homoeostasis (where all the body systems are maintained at equilibrium).

BODY MAPS

The feet (and hands) should be seen as a pair, and reflexologists look for the body map in both feet. So the right half of the body is reflected in the right foot, and the left half in the left foot. Body maps for the feet are on pages 24-25.

Single organs are found in either the right foot or the left foot or both, depending on their anatomical position. Paired organs, such as the lungs or kidneys, are found one in each foot. Exceptions include the stomach, pancreas and intestines, which are found in both feet but are not paired organs.

The central nervous system may be treated slightly

differently, as the right half of the brain controls the left side of the body and vice versa. However, a good reflexologist will always work the whole of the central nervous system. Reflexology is a holistic treatment that works the entire body, whatever initial issues the client came in with.

The position of organs and body parts is also reflected in the zones of the feet. Central organs, such as the stomach and pancreas, are usually found on the soles of both feet, towards the inside or medial edge. Outer parts of the body, such as the shoulders, are found towards the outside or lateral edge of the feet.

BASIC TECHNIQUES
There are three basic techniques used in reflexology (see page 26). Each is used for different purposes, but all three require the foot, or hand, to be held correctly in order to be effective. The hand that holds and supports the foot is called the 'holding hand', while the other (the 'working hand') gives the treatment.

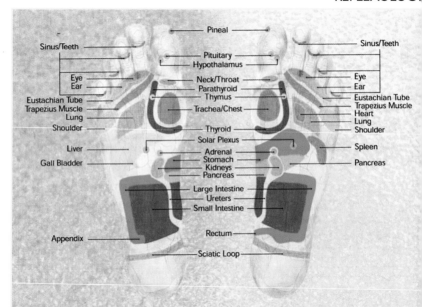

MAPS OF THE FEET

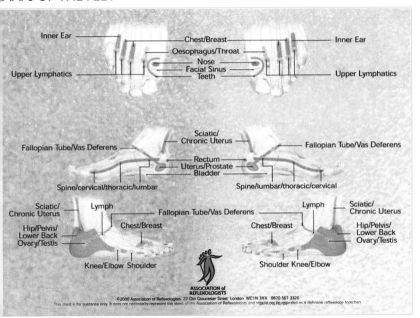

Inner Ear — Chest/Breast — Inner Ear
Upper Lymphatics — Oesophagus/Throat
Nose
Facial Sinus
Teeth — Upper Lymphatics

Sciatic/
Chronic Uterus
Fallopian Tube/Vas Deferens — Fallopian Tube/Vas Deferens
Rectum
Uterus/Prostate
Bladder
Spine/cervical/thoracic/lumbar — Spine/lumbar/thoracic/cervical

Sciatic/
Chronic Uterus — Lymph — Fallopian Tube/Vas Deferens — Lymph — Sciatic/
Chronic Uterus
Hip/Pelvis/
Lower Back
Ovary/Testis — Chest/Breast — Chest/Breast — Hip/Pelvis/
Lower Back
Ovary/Testis
Knee/Elbow Shoulder — Shoulder Knee/Elbow

**ASSOCIATION of
REFLEXOLOGISTS**

REFLEXOLOGY TECHNIQUES

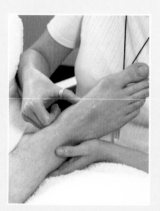

THUMB WALKING
Used to cover large areas on the bottom of the foot (see pages 50-52).

FINGER WALKING
Used to work on the tops and sides of the feet.

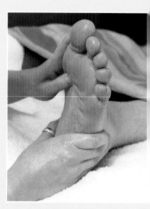

THUMB HOOK AND BACK UP
Used to apply pressure to a specific point.

LINKING

Linking is a technique that is sometimes used when an area is in need of extra attention.

For example, when treating a client with a bad right shoulder, the reflexologist may decide to link the right shoulder reflex with the left shoulder reflex, or with the hip, elbow or knee reflex. As all these are joints, they are related on an energy level.

The theory behind the technique is that linking the energies of the 'bad' shoulder with a related 'good' area aids and speeds the healing process. These relationships work both ways. So, for example, if the knee is injured, the referral area becomes the elbow.

SCIENTIFIC EXPLANATION

There have been attempts to explain the way that reflexology works using our knowledge of neurology and embryology.

We know that there are areas on the surface of the body that seem to represent internal organs. This is due to

27

the fact that the nerve supplies are related, either directly or indirectly, because their embryological development was close. The best known of these associations is probably the fact that the first sign of oxygen deprivation to heart muscle manifests as tingling or pain in the left arm. Another is shoulder-tip pain, which may be the result of an ectopic pregnancy (in which the fertilised egg fails to reach the uterus and develops in the Fallopian tube).

It seems possible that stimulation to the body's surface can, in some cases, directly affect the functioning of internal organs, although more research is needed for there to be scientifically adequate proof that there are connections between the feet and other parts of the body. While more evidence and research is being gathered and collated, some by bodies such as the Association of Reflexologists, there is already a wealth of anecdotal evidence to support that such connections exist.

Of course, it is very difficult to produce scientific evidence for something as elusive as improving health – there are so many contributing factors involved. However, one way in which we can all appreciate the effect of reflexology is through relaxation.

The majority of people who experience reflexology find it extremely relaxing, and it helps to counteract the stresses of everyday life, which allows the body to naturally rejuvenate. As stress is now widely acknowledged to be a major contributory factor in disease and ill-health, anything that reduces stress levels also reduces the opportunity for disease to develop and take hold. Consequently, reflexology can be viewed as a very effective form of preventative medicine.

4 Will Reflexology Work For Me?

First and foremost, reflexology is a therapy designed to make us feel better; to re-establish that all-important sense of well-being. As such, it is a therapy that can be of immense benefit to us all.

Reflexology can be used to treat a wide range of health problems, either in its own right or as a complement to other treatment methods.

Aside from the conditions listed on page 47 as not suitable for treatment with reflexology, therapists would argue that reflexology will always be of help to, if not a cure for, the common diseases and conditions that beset us.

The following case studies offer examples of how reflexology can be of benefit.

STRESS

Few people live stress-free lives, and for many of us the level of stress we experience daily can be very high.

Maxine is 35, and, like many women of her generation, she was trying hard to successfully juggle her career and motherhood. She worked long hours, only to come home to two boisterous young children who desperately wanted her attention, and a husband who had also been at work and was tired and in need of her attention too.

Maxine and her husband came to the point where they felt that they were losing control of the situation and decided to take stock.

A year later, they are living in a smaller, less expensive house, with no paid help. Maxine's husband now works part-time and he has taken over the housework and child-care, while Maxine works at home one day a week. Everyone has benefited from these changes.

Maxine feels that reflexology was what really helped her to take charge. At the height of their stressful-living period, Maxine had received a voucher for some reflexology, as a present from an aunt. She didn't feel she was ill, but the treatments she received made her more relaxed and able to cope.

Over a period of eight sessions she began to feel that she had the energy to face the obvious problems in her life. As she says, "Feeling better in myself made me want everyone else to feel better and to make a life for my family in which that was possible."

PREGNANCY AND CHILD-BEARING

Reflexology is a popular therapy with midwives. It is used to help with a wide range of common health problems experienced in pregnancy, labour and postnatally.

Lydia is 28. After giving birth normally to her second child, she was worried that, after four days, she had not produced any breast milk.

Lydia's midwife was also trained in reflexology, and, when she next visited Lydia, she offered her a reflexology

33

treatment.

The midwife worked on the zones for the pituitary gland, to stimulate oxytocin production (the hormone that triggers milk production). She also worked on the breast zones.

Within five minutes, Lydia felt her breasts harden and lactation began. From then onwards she experienced no problems with milk production or breast-feeding.

CANCER

Increasingly, complementary therapies are being used to support conventional cancer treatment.

In particular, these therapies are being offered to improve a patient's quality of life, and they are also used to tackle the symptoms of the cancer itself, as well as common side-effects associated with cancer treatments.

Graham is 56. He has lung cancer. He is receiving both

radiotherapy and chemotherapy, which he hopes will help him to live a little longer. However, these treatments were having an extremely debilitating effect on Graham. In addition, he was very anxious about the future, in particular about how his wife was coping.

The hospital where Graham receives his treatment employs several different complementary therapists in the cancer unit, including a massage therapist, an aromatherapist and a reflexologist. Graham was offered a course of 10 treatments of his choice, and he opted for reflexology.

As a result of the reflexology, Graham reported that he was feeling a lot more relaxed, and that he was, at last, sleeping well at night. He also said that his energy levels had increased and he was able to enjoy life more as a result.

Interestingly, Graham also said that the cancer pain he had been experiencing had decreased since he had been receiving reflexology.

TREATING CHILDREN

Reflexology is used to treat many childhood health problems, from minor infections to more serious conditions, such as asthma.

In babies, colic, teething problems and eczema can all respond well to reflexology.

Usually, children's sessions are shorter than for adults, at around 30 minutes. Parents will be invited to help keep their child comfortable and relaxed throughout the treatment.

Jenny is four years old and had suffered from glue ear (when the middle ear becomes blocked with mucus) for a year.

Jenny's mother was concerned that, while the hearing loss was small, it increased significantly every time Jenny got a cold. As Jenny is now at school full-time, her mother was worried that she would struggle to hear her teacher against the noisy back-drop of the classroom.

A friend suggested reflexology, and so an appointment was arranged with the friend's therapist.

Jenny enjoyed the treatments – and all the attention she received – and, after six sessions, her mother felt there had been a significant improvement.

At Jenny's next hearing-test appointment, the consultant was pleased to find that the glue ear had completely cleared in the right ear and was much less serious in the left.

Reflexology can be very effective for childhood illnesses, such as glue ear.

37

5 Going To A Reflexologist

Having decided that you want to try reflexology, you may be wondering what you have to do to start treatment and what to expect when you get there.

FOOT CARE

To get the best out of a reflexology treatment, therapists recommend that you ensure your feet are in as good a condition as possible beforehand. While it would be wonderful if everyone had perfect feet and followed the advice at the end of this chapter, refelxologists can work around a variety of foot problems, so do not let a minor foot problem deter you – if in doubt, ask the therapist, who will quickly tell you whether or not your foot problem is a barrier to treatment.

WHAT TO EXPECT

As with most complementary therapies, a reflexology appointment will start with a discussion of your health and lifestyle. Your therapist will want to know about you as a person – taking account not only of physical symptoms but also psychological, emotional and even spiritual aspects.

The therapist will want to establish that you do not suffer from any of the conditions that make reflexology inadvisable (see page 47), and it is important that you tell them of any medication you are taking (including natural remedies, such as homoeopathic preparations or herbal remedies), as reflexology may interfere with their action.

If your feet are to be treated, you will be asked to remove your footwear. Once you are seated or lying comfortably, the reflexologist will cleanse and dry your feet. He or she will then examine them for any initial indications of health problems.

The therapist may dust your feet with talcum powder before giving an initial massage to discover areas of tenderness or pain. Your reflexologist will respond to sensations in the feet, which

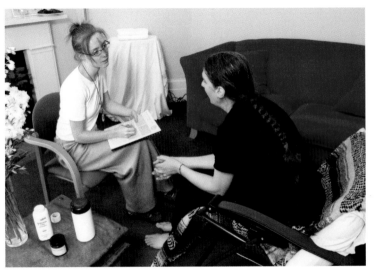

At your initial consultation, your reflexologist will want to find out as much as possible about your health history.

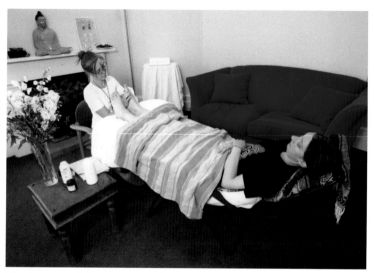

The therapist will cleanse and dry your feet before examining them for indications of ill-health.

may be described as 'granular accumulations', 'grittiness under the skin' or 'crystal deposits'. However they are described, these sensations can be said to indicate where in the body imbalances are likely to be.

THERAPY NOT DIAGNOSIS

It is important here to emphasise that reflexologists do not 'diagnose'. A good reflexologist can identify problems, but it is not within their remit to attach clinical labels to them in the way that a medical doctor would. The idea behind reflexology is to use observation and treatment therapeutically, regardless of what you – or your reflexologist – might think the problem is.

Reflexologists do not promise to treat a specific problem. Rather, they work towards helping the body help itself and producing a heightened sense of well-being.

TREATMENT

Your reflexologist would like you to be relaxed during

treatment, so they will make sure you are comfortable and warm. They may also try to create a restful ambience to help you relax. This may involve gentle music or natural sounds, good (but not harsh) lighting, and a pleasant fragrance using an essential-oil burner.

Once the reflexologist has initially assessed and wiped your feet, treatment will begin. Your therapist will support the foot with one hand and apply pressure with the other. The pressure each reflexologist uses will vary from light touch to firm and strong, although it should not be heavy. If you find it uncomfortable or painful, you should let your therapist know.

It is unusual for anyone not to be able to tolerate reflexology, however sensitive or ticklish their feet may be in different circumstances.

A standard treatment usually lasts for about an hour, although this may vary. After an hour's treatment, most people report feeling more relaxed. The number of sessions a person will need varies according to the individual, and this is something your reflexologist will discuss with you. They will also discuss ways in which you can support the treatment by leading a healthy lifestyle – including eating a healthy diet, exercising sensibly and regularly, and tackling stressful areas of your life.

At the end of the session, you may feel deeply relaxed, so take a little time before rushing off to do something else, and always remember to drink plenty of water throughout the day following a treatment.

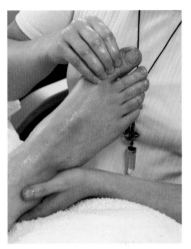

During treatment, the therapist will normally support your foot with one hand, and massage with the other hand.

45

POST-TREATMENT

While the vast majority of people find reflexology calming and relaxing, some people experience what is known as a 'healing crisis' following treatment. This is a temporary reaction, and may include the following symptoms:

- Feeling light-headed
- Feeling very cold for one or two days after a treatment
- Flu-like symptoms
- Lethargy
- Enhanced or altered sleep patterns
- Reduction in blood pressure
- Increase in excretory function.

These are rare, but if symptoms persist, medical advice should be sought.

SAFETY FIRST

Reflexology is generally considered a very safe treatment. However, in the absence of thorough research, there are certain circumstances under which it is probably best not to use reflexology. There are certain conditions that all reflexologists agree are contraindicated, such as deep vein thrombosis (blood clotting within the veins). However, contraindications also depend on the individual reflexologist. If you are concerned, discuss the matter with your doctor and therapist.

SUGGESTIONS FOR GOOD FOOT CARE

Acquiring a good foot-care routine will not only make reflexology more pleasant for your therapist, but it will also improve the condition of your feet and help to avoid future problems. A good routine should involve:

- Drying your feet carefully after washing – especially between the toes. Residual moisture is the perfect setting for fungal infections, such as athlete's foot.
- Keep your skin smooth and soft by using a pumice stone in the bath, or a mildly abrasive foot cream.
- Toenails should be kept short and cut straight across, rather than in a curve, as this helps to prevent nails in-growing.
- Moisturise regularly.

6 Self Help

It is extremely difficult to practise reflexology on your own feet, but there are a number of self-help avenues you can take advantage of.

CAUTION
There are several products on the market that are said to stimulate the reflexes, and that are designed for self-help purposes. These include reflexology shoes, mats, rollers and brushes. However, used unsupervised, these can do more harm than good.

Overused, or used inappropriately, these products – especially the shoes – can overstimulate the reflexes. It is better to seek the help of a trained reflexologist.

HAND REFLEXOLOGY
Self-help hand reflexology is no substitute for proper treatment by a trained therapist. If you have an exisiting problem, or you find an area of concern when practising hand reflexology, it is advisable to consult a qualified reflexologist.

However, practised at home as a means of maintaining health, a simple form of self-applied hand reflexology can be very beneficial. All you need is a comfortable chair and a cushion to support your lower arms.

You should spend about 10 minutes working on each hand, using the sequence given on pages 56-59. Start with your right hand first, and then follow with your left.

THUMB WALKING

Before you start, you will need to practise the technique of thumb walking, in order for your treatment to be effective.

While sitting comfortably, with your hands supported, place your thumb on the area of your other hand to be treated (1). Then flex the first joint of the thumb to apply a precise point of pressure directly to the area your thumb is in touch with, with your thumb at a 45-degree angle (2). Then straighten your thumb, relaxing the pressure without losing contact with the skin (3). Repeat this flexing

THUMB WALKING

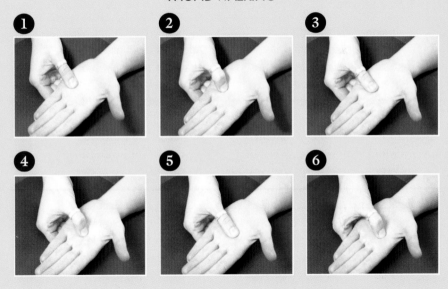

and releasing to allow your thumb to move forwards, making it 'walk' (4-6). A forward movement will automatically occur by the pressure-relaxation movement, so there is no need to force it.

You can also experiment with finger walking, which is very similar, except that you use your index finger instead of your thumb.

You can exert pressure in reflexology through the use of leverage – by using your four fingers in opposition to your thumb.

Constant pressure is essential when thumb walking, and you should practise this technique regularly until you do not feel any on-off-on-off pressure at each bend of the thumb.

Once you are satisfied that you can thumb walk correctly, you can have a go at the sequence described on pages 56-59.

To orientate yourself to the reflexes referred to, have a copy of the hand reflexes nearby (see pages 53-55).

REFLEXOLOGY POINTS ON THE BACK OF THE HAND

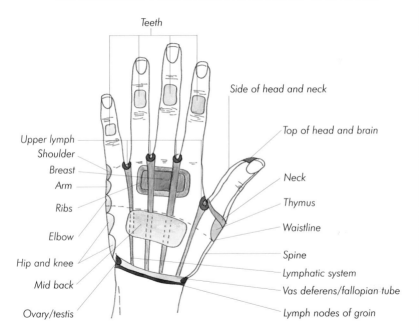

Teeth

Side of head and neck

Top of head and brain

Upper lymph
Shoulder
Breast
Arm

Ribs

Elbow

Hip and knee

Mid back

Ovary/testis

Neck

Thymus

Waistline

Spine

Lymphatic system

Vas deferens/fallopian tube

Lymph nodes of groin

REFLEXOLOGY POINTS ON THE LEFT PALM

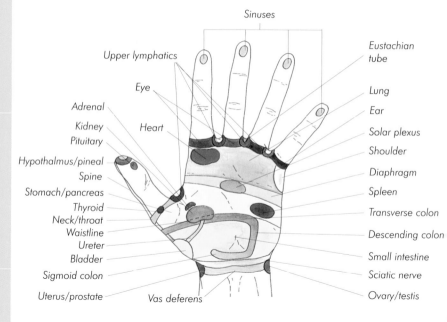

Sinuses

Upper lymphatics

Eye

Adrenal
Kidney
Pituitary
Hypothalmus/pineal
Spine
Stomach/pancreas
Thyroid
Neck/throat
Waistline
Ureter
Bladder
Sigmoid colon
Uterus/prostate

Heart

Vas deferens

Eustachian tube

Lung
Ear
Solar plexus
Shoulder
Diaphragm
Spleen
Transverse colon
Descending colon
Small intestine
Sciatic nerve
Ovary/testis

54

REFLEXOLOGY POINTS ON THE RIGHT PALM

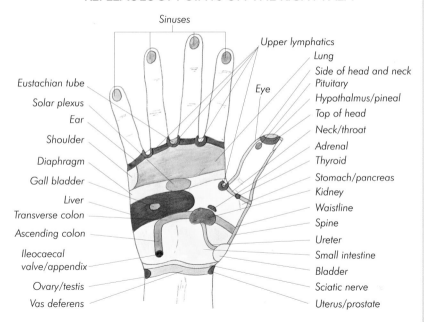

Sinuses

Upper lymphatics

Lung

Side of head and neck

Pituitary

Hypothalmus/pineal

Eye

Top of head

Neck/throat

Adrenal

Thyroid

Stomach/pancreas

Kidney

Waistline

Spine

Ureter

Small intestine

Bladder

Sciatic nerve

Uterus/prostate

Eustachian tube

Solar plexus

Ear

Shoulder

Diaphragm

Gall bladder

Liver

Transverse colon

Ascending colon

Ileocaecal valve/appendix

Ovary/testis

Vas deferens

SPINE
Thumb walk up and then down the spine reflex at the side of the thumb.

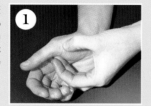

TEETH AND SINUSES
Thumb walk up and down the fingers. The teeth reflexes are on the tops of the fingers, and the sinus reflexes are on the palm side of the fingers.

HEAD AND NECK
Thumb walk up and down the head reflex. This is on both sides of the thumb. Go across the base of the thumb on both hands for the neck.

SHOULDERS
Thumb walk and hold at the base of the little finger, especially towards the outer side of the hand. Shoulder reflexes are found on both hands.

TREATMENT ROUTINE
then treat the other)

LUNGS
Work across all the finger bases, on the opposite side of the knuckles. Treat both hands.

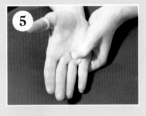

DIAPHRAGM AND SOLAR PLEXUS
Thumb walk along the 'line' running across the hands at the base of the lung area (at the root of the finger joints). The solar plexus is found at the root of the first two fingers; hook up into this area and hold it for a moment.

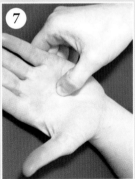

LIVER AND SPLEEN
The liver is found on the right hand, under the diaphragm, predominantly below the little and two middle fingers. The spleen is found in the same place on the left hand, though only under the little and next finger. Thumb walk over these areas.

STOMACH

This is found on both hands, although predominantly on the left. It is found under the diaphragm, under the thumb and first two fingers. On the right hand it is under the thumb only. Thumb walk these areas.

INTESTINES

Thumb walk over the intestines, which are found on both hands below the thumb and all the fingers.

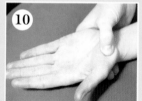

BLADDER

Hold this reflex for a moment or two. It is found at the side of the thumb joint on both hands.

KIDNEYS AND URETER

Each kidney is reflected in each hand. Thumb walk along the ureter from the bladder, across the thumb joint towards the fingers, staying in line with the gap between the first two fingers. Stop when you are in line with the 'top' of the thumb – this area is the kidney reflex. Hook into this point and hold for a moment.

OVARIES AND UTERUS/TESTES AND PROSTATE

These are found on both hands. The ovaries/testes are found on the outer edge of the hand, just above the wrist. The uterus/prostate is in the same place on the inner edge of the hand.

LYMPHATIC SYSTEM

This is found across the top/back of the hands, and it is very important to finish a treatment routine with this. There is so much involved in the lymphatic system that it is best to work across the whole of the hands, paying particular attention to the areas between the fingers and between the fingers and thumb.

AND FINALLY...

To finish your self-help treatment routine, gently rub and smooth over your whole hands and lightly hold them for a moment. Then have a glass of water.

Further Information

The following contact details will help you to find a qualified reflexologist practitioner in your area.

ASSOCIATION OF
REFLEXOLOGISTS
27 Old Gloucester Street
London
WC1N 3XX
Tel: 0870 5673320
Web: www.aor.org.uk

BRITISH REFLEXOLOGY
ASSOCIATION
Monks Orchard
Whitbourne
Worcester
WR6 5RB
Tel: 01886 821207
Web: www.britreflex.co.uk

INTERNATIONAL
FEDERATION OF
REFLEXOLOGISTS
76-78 Edridge Road

Croydon
Surrey
CR0 1EF
Tel: 020 8667 9458
Web: www.reflexology-ifr.com

REFLEXOLOGY FORUM
PO Box 2367
South Croydon
Surrey
CR2 7ZE

Please ensure that your practitioner is professionally qualified, has insurance and is a member of a bonafide organisation.

About the author

Joanna Trevelyan is an experienced journalist with a particular interest in complementary therapies, health and nursing, environmental health issues, and women's issues. She has written for a wide range of professional bodies, including the World Health Organisation, the Natural Medicines Society, the Parliamentary Group for Complementary and Alternative Medicine, and the Foundation for Integrated Health. Joanna has also been the editor of the professional journal *Nursing Times*. In 1994, she was awarded a Commendation in the Medical Journalism Awards.

CONSULTANT
Special thanks are due to Samantha Beeson (Manth), the consultant reflexologist in the photographs, who edited the factual content of this book. Manth is an accredited member of the Association of Reflexologists, who continues to further her knowledge through postgraduate studies. She is one of the core founders of Bodymind Complementary Health in London, and she organises healing areas for annual festivals. Manth can be contacted through her website: www.viryatreatments.co.uk

ACKNOWLEDGEMENTS
The publisher would like to extend thanks to the Association of Reflexologists for the foot charts on pages 24-25, Sylvia De Medfort-Dunn (Metamorphic Association) for her help with Metamorphic Reflexology on pages 17-18, and Dick Smith (for photography).

Other titles in the series

- Understanding Acupressure
- Understanding Acupuncture
- Understanding The Alexander Technique
- Understanding Aloe Vera
- Understanding Aromatherapy
- Understanding Bach Flower Remedies
- Understanding The Bowen Technique
- Understanding Craniosacral Therapy
- Understanding Echinacea
- Understanding Evening Primrose
- Understanding Fish Oils
- Understanding Garlic
- Understanding Ginseng
- Understanding Head Massage
- Understanding Kinesiology
- Understanding Lavender
- Understanding Massage
- Understanding Pilates
- Understanding Reiki
- Understanding St. John's Wort
- Understanding Shiatsu
- Understanding Yoga

First published 2005 by First Stone Publishing
PO Box 8, Lydney, Gloucestershire, GL15 6YD

The contents of this book are for information only and are not intended as a substitute for appropriate medical attention. The author and publishers admit no liability for any consequences arising from following any advice contained within this book. If you have any concerns about your health or medication, always consult your doctor.

ISBN 1 904439 31 4

Printed and bound in Hong Kong through Printworks International Ltd.